入门篇
我的英语日记书

主编：清瑶
编委：宝洛尔

超有趣的英语日记书！

北京理工大学出版社

版权专有　侵权必究

图书在版编目（CIP）数据

我的英语日记书．入门篇 / 清瑶主编．— 北京：北京理工大学出版社，2019.9

ISBN 978-7-5682-7555-2

Ⅰ．①我… Ⅱ．①清… Ⅲ．①英语 – 日记 – 写作 – 小学 – 教学参考资料 Ⅳ．① G624.313

中国版本图书馆 CIP 数据核字（2019）第 197281 号

出版发行 / 北京理工大学出版社有限责任公司
社　　址 / 北京市海淀区中关村南大街 5 号
邮　　编 / 100081
电　　话 /（010）68914775（总编室）
　　　　　（010）82562903（教材售后服务热线）
　　　　　（010）68948351（其他图书服务热线）
网　　址 / http://www.bitpress.com.cn
经　　销 / 全国各地新华书店
印　　刷 / 天津东辰丰彩印刷有限公司
开　　本 / 710 毫米 × 1000 毫米　1/16　　　　责任编辑 / 赵兰辉
印　　张 / 10　　　　　　　　　　　　　　　　文案编辑 / 李文文
字　　数 / 112 千字　　　　　　　　　　　　　 责任校对 / 周瑞红
版　　次 / 2019 年 9 月第 1 版　2019 年 9 月第 1 次印刷　责任印制 / 施胜娟
定　　价 / 32.80 元

图书出现印装质量问题，请拨打售后服务热线，本社负责调换

前言

　　《英语课程标准》对基础教育阶段听、说、读、写四个技能提出了九个级别的目标要求，其中在语言技能（听说读写）二级"写"的目标描述中明确要求："小学生能模仿范例写句子；能写出简单的问候语；能根据要求为图片、实物等写出简短的标题或描述；能基本正确地使用大小写字母和标点符号。"

　　英语写作教学是小学英语教学中非常重要的部分，贯穿整个教学过程。写作教学对帮助学生了解英语思维的方式，养成运用英语思维进行思考的习惯，提高学生综合运用语言知识的能力大有益处。

　　本套丛书旨在为初学英语的小学生在英语写作方面提供一些指导和帮助。本书分为5个单元，每个单元一个话题，话题围绕小学生的日常生活展开。通过"好词妙妙屋—语法小贴士—语法大擂台—日记导图秀—参考范文—词汇加油站"等栏目，由浅入深、循序渐进地进行训练，帮助学生正确地使用词汇，锻炼学生组织句子的能力。每篇日记都是一个小故事，并配上有趣的图片，帮助小学生理解日记内容，图文并茂，趣味盎然。"日记导图秀"栏目设置了提示性问题，能有效地帮助学生写出相应话题的段落；"语法小贴士"栏目为小学生提供相应的语法辅导，帮助学生们运用正确的句式进行写作训练。

  我们衷心地希望本套丛书能够帮助小学生更好地掌握英语写作的方法，使学生们不断提高英语成绩。本套丛书必然还存在很多需要改进之处，恳请读者批评指正，更望专家不吝赐教。

目录 Contents

Unit 1
My Family and Friends

1. This Is Me! — 002
2. My Family — 008
3. My Grandpa's Birthday — 013
4. My Best Friend—Xiao Ming — 019
5. Teachers' Day — 025

Unit 2
Places

6. My Room — 032
7. On the Farm — 038
8. My Hometown — 044
9. A Trip in Hangzhou — 049
10. On My Way to School — 055

Unit 3
School Life

11. An Interesting English Class — 062
12. Sports Meeting — 068
13. The Tug of War — 074
14. A Painting Exhibition — 080
15. Spring Outing — 085

目录 Contents

Unit 4 Trips

16.	I Went to Harbin	092
17.	How to Travel	098
18.	The Forbidden City	104
19.	I Got Lost!	110
20.	Preparing for a Trip	115

Unit 5 Activities

21.	My Day	122
22.	A Football Match	128
23.	Planting Trees	133
24.	Preparing for Christmas	138
25.	I Can Shop	143

Unit 1

My Family and Friends

1. This Is Me!

June 2nd　　　　**Thursday**　　　　**Rainy**

Hello, everyone! My name is Dobby Black. I'm ten years old, and I'm a boy.

I'm from Australia, and now I live in Shanghai with my family.

I am a student in a primary school. I like playing basketball with my classmates after class. I love my classmates very much.

This is me! Do you like me?

My Family and Friends

UNIT 1

好词妙妙屋

name 名字 boy 男孩 Australia 澳大利亚
live 居住 family 家人 student 学生
classmate 同学 love 喜爱

be from 来自 play basketball 打篮球
primary school 小学 after class 课后

参考译文

6月2日　　　　星期四　　　　　　雨

大家好！我的名字是多比·布莱克。我今年10岁，是一个男孩。

我来自澳大利亚，我现在和我的家人住在上海。

我是一名小学生。我喜欢放学后和我的同学一起打篮球。我非常喜欢我的同学。

这就是我！你们喜欢我吗？

语法小贴士

多比来到中国后认识了许多小伙伴，他们每个人都有自己的名字。他身边的事物也都有名称，他所吃的食物和看到的动物也都有名字。我们把这些表示人名、事物、食物、动物等名称的词统一称为名词。

这些名词有的能数得过来，如：鸭子、树、桌子等；而有些东西却无法计数，比如空气、水、牛奶等。在英语中，我们把这些能数得出个数的名词叫作可数名词，而不可计量的名词叫作不可数名词。

可数名词

boy　　　　　girl　　　　　star　　　　　tree

flower　　　　desk　　　　monkey　　　　skirt

不可数名词

milk　　　　juice　　　　coffee　　　　rice

bread　　　　paper　　　　meat　　　　cheese

My Family and Friends

UNIT 1

语法大擂台

读一读下面的单词，请把它们送回各自的家。

rain   bag   snow   water

book   cake   tea   pencil

cap   cat   money   ice

可数名词

不可数名词

日记导图秀

小朋友，请你模仿上面的日记写一篇关于自己的日记吧！

外貌：
tall, thin

性格：
kind, shy

爱好：
play basketball

国籍：
Chinese, American

_____(DATE)　_____(DAY)　_____(WEATHER)

This Is Me!

UNIT 1 My Family and Friends

参考范文

| June 22nd | Saturday | Sunny |

This Is Me!

Hello, everyone! My name is Lucy. I'm tall and thin. I'm from England. I am a student in a primary school. I like dancing. Every Sunday, I go to the dancing class. This is me! Do you like me?

词汇加油站

> 描写外貌：

fat 胖的　　　　　　short 矮的
big 大的　　　　　　small 小的

> 描写兴趣爱好：

run 跑步　　　　　　sing 唱歌
swim 游泳　　　　　dance 跳舞
play football 踢足球　play the piano 弹钢琴

> 描写性格：

outgoing 外向的　　　warm-hearted 热心的

2. My Family

April 4th   **Thursday**   **Sunny**

My family is big. There are six people in my family. They are my parents, my grandparents, my little sister Amy and I. Oh, I also have a lovely dog, Poppy.

My father is 45 years old, and he is a driver. My mother is 44 years old, and she is a nurse. My grandparents are retired now. My little sister is only three years old.

We have a happy family. We love each other very much!

My Family and Friends

UNIT 1

好词妙妙屋

family 家庭　　　parents 爸爸妈妈　　　grandparents 爷爷奶奶
sister 妹妹　　　lovely 可爱的　　　　father 爸爸
driver 司机　　　mother 妈妈　　　　nurse 护士
retired 退休的

each other 互相，彼此　　　　　very much 非常
There be... 有……

参考译文

4月4日　　　　　星期四　　　　　晴

　　我有一个大家庭。家里有爸爸妈妈、爷爷奶奶、我的小妹妹艾米和我，共6口人。哦，我还有一只可爱的小狗——波比。

　　我的爸爸45岁，他是一位司机。我的妈妈44岁，她是一名护士。我的爷爷奶奶已经退休了，我的妹妹今年只有3岁。

　　我们有一个非常幸福的家庭，我们非常爱彼此！

语法小贴士

　　在英语中，名词分为可数名词和不可数名词。只提到一个可数名词时，用单数形式，提到两个或两个以上可数名词时，就要用名词的复数形式了。在通常情况下，可数名词变为复数时就在词尾加 -s。我有一只小狗，所以小狗用单数，我的爸爸妈妈是两个人，所以用复数。

a cat　　　two cats　　　an apple　　　some apples

a panda　　　five pandas　　　a bed　　　two beds

a hand　　　two hands　　　a bag　　　five bags

语法大擂台

请写出下列单词的复数形式。

banana _____　　car _____　　pen _____

eraser _____　　eye _____　　shoe _____

door _____　　orange _____　　book _____

picture _____　　computer _____　　head _____

My Family and Friends

UNIT 1

日记导图秀

小朋友，你的家里都有哪些人呢？他们分别是谁，做什么工作？请你模仿上面的日记写一篇关于你的家庭的日记吧！

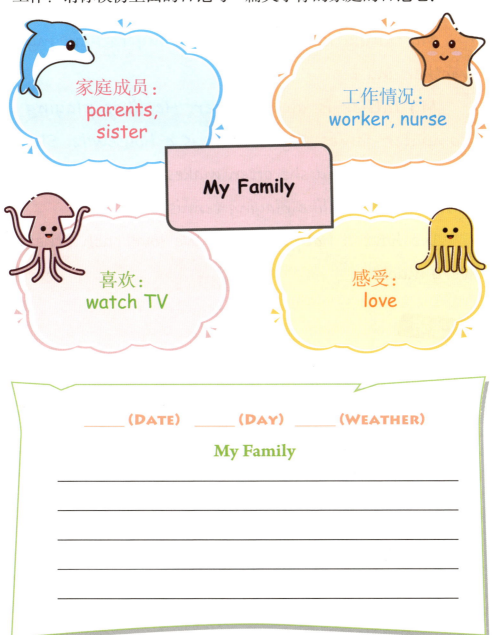

家庭成员：
parents, sister

工作情况：
worker, nurse

My Family

喜欢：
watch TV

感受：
love

_____ (Date) _____ (Day) _____ (Weather)

My Family

_____

_____

_____

_____

_____

参考范文

January 15th　　　　Tuesday　　　　Snowy

My Family

My family is small. There is my father, my mother and I.

My father is an engineer. He likes playing computer games. My mother is a housewife. She likes cooking, and she often makes delicious food. I am a student. I like playing tennis.

We have a happy family. We love each other very much!

词汇加油站

▶ 描写家庭成员：

There are... people in my family. 我家有……口人。

father 爸爸　　　　mother 妈妈
grandfather 爷爷　　grandmother 奶奶
sister 姐姐／妹妹　　brother 哥哥／弟弟

▶ 描写职业：

worker 工人　　doctor 医生　　teacher 老师
police 警察　　chef 厨师

My Family and Friends

UNIT 1

3. My Grandpa's Birthday

| May 25th | Saturday | Cloudy |

Today is my grandpa's birthday. He's already 70 years old. We are going to hold a birthday party for him.

Grandpa likes playing chess, so Dad will give him a set of chess as a birthday gift. Mom is making a birthday cake in the kitchen. Grandma is making dishes. Amy and I are making a birthday card for him.

We are very busy. We all hope grandpa will be happy for ever.

好词妙妙屋

birthday 生日
chess 象棋
card 卡片

already 已经
gift 礼物
busy 忙碌

hold 举办
kitchen 厨房
happy 快乐

be going to 将要
a set of 一套

birthday party 生日会
make dishes 做饭

play chess 下象棋
for ever 永远

参考译文

5月25日　　　　　星期六　　　　　　多云

今天是我爷爷的生日。他已经70岁了。我们准备给他举办一个生日会。

爷爷喜欢下象棋，所以爸爸准备送他一套象棋作为生日礼物。妈妈在厨房做生日蛋糕。奶奶在做菜。艾米和我在给他做生日贺卡。

我们都很忙。我们希望爷爷能永远开心。

语法小贴士

小朋友们，你们已经知道英语中名词变复数的基本规则了，但是有些单词比较淘气，不愿意遵循这个基本规则。那该怎么办呢？遇到这些不守规则的单词该如何处理呢？我们今天就来学习一下这些不守规则的单词如何变成复数。小朋友们先看一下这几组单词。

My Family and Friends

UNIT 1

第一组

a bus 一辆公共汽车　　two buses 两辆公共汽车
a box 一个盒子　　　　five boxes 五个盒子
a brush 一只刷子　　　three brushes 三只刷子
a watch 一块手表　　　two watches 两块手表

第二组

a family 一个家庭　　two families 两个家庭
a baby 一个小孩　　　three babies 三个小孩
a boy 一个男孩　　　　five boys 五个男孩
a toy 一个玩具　　　　two toys 两个玩具

第三组

a knife 一把刀　　　two knives 两把刀
a leaf 一片树叶　　three leaves 三片树叶

小朋友，你发现上面三组单词的变化规则了吗？这些淘气的单词虽然不遵守常规，但是他们还是有规律可循的，下面我们就来看一看。

在第一组单词中，我们发现，以 s, x, sh, ch 结尾的单词，在变复数的时候，在词尾加 -es。

这样的单词还有：fox — foxes 狐狸，glass — glasses 玻璃杯

在第二组单词中，我们发现，以 y 结尾的单词中，如果 y 前面的字母是元音字母，变复数时在词尾直接加 -s，如果 y 前面的字母是辅音，就需要把 y 变成 i，再加 -es。

这样的单词还有：factory — factories 工厂

在第三组单词中，我们发现，以 f 或 fe 结尾的单词，在变复数的时候，要把 f 或 fe 变成 v，再加 -es。

这样的单词还有：life — lives 生命　　wolf — wolves 狼

语法大擂台

读一读下面的单词，请把它们送回各自的家。

bus	lady	monkey
wife	friend	cake
shelf	cherry	match
thief	life	dress
toothbrush	sport	holiday

加 -s

变 y 为 i，再加 -es

加 -es

变 f 或 fe 为 v，再加 -es

My Family and Friends

UNIT 1

日记导图秀

小朋友，你有没有参加过生日会？或者给你的家人举办过生日会？请你模仿上面的日记写一篇关于你家人的生日的日记吧！

生日：
40 years old

准备：
gift

My _____'s
Birthday

原因：
busy

表达感情：
love

_____ (DATE) _____ (DAY) _____ (WEATHER)

My _____'s Birthday

参考范文

March 3rd　　　　Saturday　　　　Windy

My Father's Birthday

Today is my father's birthday. We are going to hold a birthday party for him.

My father likes collecting watches very much, so my mother will give him a watch as a birthday gift. I will make a birthday card for him.

I love my father very much. We hope he will be happy for ever.

词汇加油站

▶ 在生日会前你可能会做：

　　clean the house 打扫房间

　　decorate the room 装饰屋子

　　make a birthday cake 做生日蛋糕

　　buy / make birthday present 买 / 做生日礼物

▶ 在生日会上大家可能会做：

　　have a big meal 吃一顿大餐

　　sing songs and dance 唱歌跳舞

　　play games 做游戏

　　send birthday presents 送生日礼物

My Family and Friends

UNIT 1

4. My Best Friend—Xiao Ming

| June 24th | Monday | Windy |

My best friend is Xiao Ming. He is also my deskmate. He is tall and thin.

He is very kind and friendly, and he often helps me with my Chinese. My English is better than his, so I often help him with his English.

We get along very well with each other!

好词妙妙屋

deskmate 同桌
thin 瘦的
friendly 友好的

tall 高的
kind 善良的
Chinese 汉语

help... with 帮助
get along with 与……相处

better than 比……好

参考译文

6月24日　　　　星期一　　　　风

　　我最好的朋友叫肖明。他也是我的同桌。他又高又瘦。他非常善良友好，经常帮我学习语文。我的英语比他好，所以我经常帮他学习英语。

　　我们相处得非常好！

My Family and Friends

UNIT 1

语法·小贴士

学习了名词变复数的一般规则，也掌握了一些名词变复数的特殊规则，可是肖明发现还有一些淘气的单词无法归类，他们的单复数差异特别大，很难记忆。他向多比请教方法，但多比也没有好的办法，只能一个一个记忆。这样的单词有哪些呢？

单数	复数	中文释义
tooth	teeth	牙齿
mouse	mice	老鼠
goose	geese	鹅
foot	feet	脚
man	men	男人
woman	women	女人
child	children	小孩

以上这些单词的复数形式，小朋友们一定要多记忆，这样以后遇到他们的时候就能知道他们的意思了，阅读时就不会有障碍了。

想一想：你们还知道哪些单词的单复数差异比较大吗？请你和同学们交流下吧！

语法大擂台

读一读下面的单词，请把它们与其对应的图片连线。

1. geese

A.

2. child

B.

3. teeth

C.

4. mice

D.

5. man

E.

My Family and Friends

UNIT 1

日记导图秀

小朋友，你最好的朋友是谁呢？他有哪些特点？请你模仿上面的日记写一篇关于他的日记吧！

外貌：
tall, thin

性格：
kind, shy

My Friend

擅长：
play basketball

来自：
China, America

_____(DATE) _____(DAY) _____(WEATHER)

My Friend

_____
_____
_____
_____
_____

参考范文

February 12th　　　Monday　　　Snowy

My Friend

　　I have a good friend. His name is Daming. He is from Sichuan, China. He is short and thin.

　　He is very nice. He always helps others with their studies.

　　He is good at running. He won the first place in our last sports meeting.

　　We get along very well with each other!

词汇加油站

> 描写外貌：

　　fat 胖的　　　　short 矮的　　　　beautiful 漂亮的
　　pretty 漂亮的　　straight 直的　　　long 长的

> 描写兴趣爱好：

　　good at 擅长　　　swim 游泳　　　dance 跳舞
　　play football 踢足球　　　play the piano 弹钢琴

> 描写性格：

　　hard-working 勤奋的　　　warm-hearted 热心的
　　friendly 友好的　　　　　honest 诚实的

My Family and Friends

UNIT 1

 ## 5. Teachers' Day

September 11th　　　**Wednesday**　　　**Foggy**

Yesterday was Teachers' Day. It was a great day for all the teachers.

We wanted to thank our teachers. In the morning, we cleaned the classroom. Our monitor bought some flowers. In the afternoon, we held a party. We sang and danced with our teachers.

We said to our teachers, "Thank you!" We had a very happy day!

好词妙妙屋

great 美好的   thank 感谢   monitor 班长
buy 买（过去式为 bought）   party 聚会

clean the classroom 打扫教室   hold a party 举办聚会
sing and dance 唱歌跳舞

参考译文

9月11日　　　　　星期三　　　　　　　　雾

昨天是教师节。对所有老师来说，这是一个美好的节日。

我们想感谢我们的老师。上午，我们打扫了教室。班长还给老师买了鲜花。下午，我们举办了聚会，我们和老师一起唱歌跳舞。

我们对老师说："谢谢你们！"我们度过了非常快乐的一天。

语法小贴士

我们在汉语中经常用到"你""我""他"，那么在英语中也有这样的词，我们称为"人称代词"。英语中的人称代词有表示"我"的 I、表示"你；你们"的 you、表示"他；她；它"的 he / she / it、表示"我们"的 we、表示"他们"的 they。下面我们来认识一下这些词吧！

My Family and Friends

UNIT 1

I 我

My name is Dobby. I am 10 years old.
我叫多比。我今年 10 岁。

I am a student, and I love sports.
我是一名学生,我喜欢运动。

she 她

My mother is a nurse. She is 44 years old.
我的妈妈是一位护士。她今年 44 岁。

I have a good friend. She lives in China.
我有一个好朋友。她住在中国。

he 他

My father is a driver. He is 45 years old.
我的爸爸是一名司机。他今年 45 岁。

This is my brother. He is three years old.
这是我弟弟,他今年 3 岁。

it 它

I have a dog. It is Poppy.
我有一只小狗。它是波比。

This is my pet cat. It is very clever.
这是我的宠物猫。它非常聪明。

they 他们

My grandparents live with us. They are retired.
我的爷爷奶奶和我们住在一起。他们退休了。

I have two new friends. They are twins.
我有两个新朋友。她们是双胞胎。

we 我们

We live happily.
我们生活得很快乐。

We are going to have a sports meeting.
我们将要举办一次运动会。

语法大擂台

根据句意，选择正确的人称代词。

1. This is our English teacher, Miss Liu. _____ is a good teacher.
2. Last winter holiday, Xiao Ming and his family went to Qingdao. _____ had a good time!
3. Yesterday was my grandpa's birthday. _____ had a happy birthday.
4. _____ am a boy from Australia.
5. Today, my friends and I will go to the zoo. I hope _____ will have a good day.
6. Xiao Ming has a new pet. _____ is a cat.

My Family and Friends

UNIT 1

日记导图秀

小朋友，你知道母亲节是哪一天吗？在母亲节那天，你会如何表达自己对妈妈的感激之情？请你模仿上面的日记写一篇关于母亲节的日记吧！

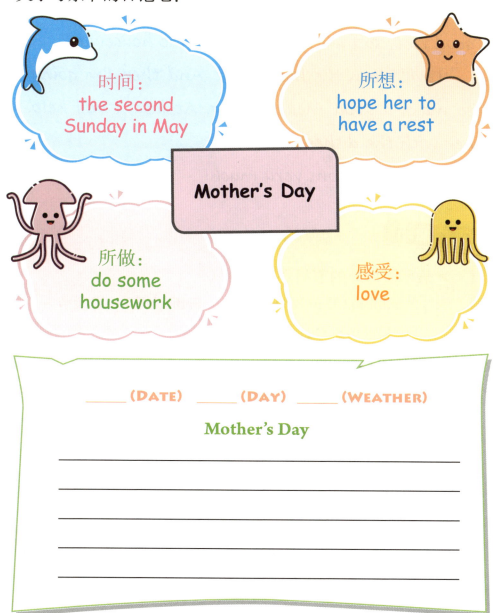

时间：the second Sunday in May

所想：hope her to have a rest

Mother's Day

所做：do some housework

感受：love

_____(DATE) _____(DAY) _____(WEATHER)

Mother's Day

_____
_____
_____
_____
_____

参考范文

| May 11th | Sunday | Sunny |

Mother's Day

Today is Mother's Day. I hope she will have a good rest, so I am going to do some housework.

I will clean the house first. And then I'm going to make a good meal for her. At last, I will help her with the dishes.

I love my mom very much!

词汇加油站

> **表示国内外的节日还有:**

National Day 国庆节　　Father's Day 父亲节
Christmas Day 圣诞节
Mid-Autumn Festival 中秋节

> **描写做家务还可能用到:**

wash clothes 洗衣服　　clean the room 打扫房间
wash dishes 洗碗　　　cook dinner 做饭

> **在节日里还可以做:**

make a card 制作卡片　　buy flowers 买花
pick up a present 挑选礼物
eat delicious food 吃美食

Unit 2

Places

6. My Room

June 22nd   Saturday   Sunny

Look! This is my room. It is very clean and tidy.

There are some books on the bookshelf. I love reading books very much. On the desk there is a photo of my family. There is a basketball under the bed. I often play basketball with my friends.

The window in my room is big and bright. I can see beautiful sights from it.

Places

UNIT 2

好词妙妙屋

clean 干净的　　　　tidy 整洁的　　　　bookshelf 书架
under 在……下面　　often 经常　　　　window 窗户
bright 明亮的

read books 看书　　　　　　a photo of my family 一张我的全家福
play basketball 打篮球　　　beautiful sights 美景

参考译文

6月22日　　　　　　星期六　　　　　　　　晴

看！这是我的房间。它又干净又整洁。

书架上有一些书，我非常喜欢看书。书桌上有一张我的全家福。床底下有一个篮球。我经常和朋友一起打篮球。

我房间的窗户又大又明亮。我通过它可以看到很多美景。

语法小贴士

我们说话的时候，常用"这个""那个"代替前面已经提到过的事物，这样的代词叫作"指示代词"。在英语中，指示代词有四个，分别是 this（这个）、that（那个）和 these（这些）、those（那些）。今天，我们来学习一下这四个单词吧！

指代近处的事物用 this 或 these，this 表示单数，these 表示复数。如：

This is a book. 这是一本书。

These are their books. 这些是他们的书。

指代远处的事物用 that 或 those，that 表示单数，those 表示复数。如：

That is my bike. 那是我的自行车。

Those are our bikes. 那些是我们的自行车。

Unit 2 Places

语法大擂台

根据所给图片，选择正确的指示代词。

this　　that　　these　　those

1. _____ is a panda. It likes eating bamboos.

2. _____ are sheep. They are eating grass.

3. _____ is my friend Jane. She is skipping.

4. _____ are my story books. I like them very much.

日记导图秀

小朋友，你有自己的房间吗？请你以日记的形式描述一下你的房间吧！

_____ (Date) _____ (Day) _____ (Weather)

My Room

_____
_____
_____
_____
_____

UNIT 2 Places

参考范文

April 14th   Thursday   Sunny

My Room

My room is a little small but tidy.

There is a bed, a desk, a chair, and a bookshelf in my room. A clock is on the desk. It often wakes me to get up. There is a dog under my chair. It is my friend.

This is my room. Do you like it?

词汇加油站

▶ 描写房间的整体状况：

　　big 大的　　　small 小的
　　clean 干净的　messy 凌乱的

▶ 房间里的家具还有：

　　bookcase 书柜　chair 椅子　table 桌子

▶ 描写位置：

　　near 在……附近　under 在……下面
　　beside 在……旁边　behind 在……后面

7. On the Farm

August 11th   **Sunday**   **Sunny**

Today I went to the farm with my parents and my little sister Amy. It is very big. And there are lots of animals and plants in it.

In the morning, we helped feed the sheep and cows. This was our first time to feed animals, so it was very interesting. In the afternoon, we helped water the grapes.

We went home at five. We were very tired but happy.

Places

UNIT 2

好词妙妙屋

farm 农场
animal 动物
help 帮忙
sheep 绵羊
interesting 有趣的
grape 葡萄

go 去（过去式为 went）
plant 植物
feed 喂
cow 奶牛
water 浇水
tired 累的

go to the farm 去农场
feed animals 喂动物

first time 第一次
go home 回家

参考译文

8月11日　　　　　星期日　　　　　晴

　　我今天和爸爸妈妈、妹妹艾米一起去农场了。农场非常大，里面有许多动物和植物。

　　上午，我们帮忙喂绵羊和奶牛。这是我们第一次喂动物，所以非常有趣。下午，我们帮忙给葡萄浇水。

　　我们下午五点回家了。我们虽然很累但很开心。

语法小贴士

小朋友们都知道，汉语中表示单个物体时可以用"一"，在英语中除了用 one 表示"一"外，还有其他表达方式吗？当然有啦！在英语中，我们把这类表示"一"的词称为冠词。我们先看看下面几个例子。

a book 一本书 　　　　a desk 一张桌子
a pear 一个梨　　　　　a banana 一根香蕉
an apple 一个苹果　　　an orange 一个橙子
an egg 一个鸡蛋　　　　an eraser 一块橡皮

通过上面的例子，小朋友们发现什么规律了吗？哪些单词前用 a？哪些单词前用 an？

我们发现，单词 book, desk, pear, banana 都是以辅音发音开头的，而单词 apple, orange, egg, eraser 都是以元音发音开头的，因此我们可以总结如下：

冠词 a 用在以辅音发音开头的单词前，冠词 an 用在以元音发音开头的单词前。

Places

UNIT 2

语法大擂台

读一读下面的单词，请把它们送回各自的家。

grape   corn   orange   map

airplane   tomato   ear   elephant

lion   actor   tree   ant

a   an

日记导图秀

小朋友，你去过公园吗？请你模仿上面的日记写一篇关于公园的日记吧！

_____ (DATE) _____ (DAY) _____ (WEATHER)

In the Park

UNIT 2 Places

参考范文

April 21st　　　**Sunday**　　　**Sunny**

In the Park

There is a park in the center of our city. It is very beautiful.

Today is Sunday. I went to the park with my friends. In the park, we did our homework first. Then Judy and Kate went boating. Cindy and I flew kites. At noon, we had a picnic together.

We had a happy day!

词汇加油站

> 描写公园你可能会用到：

gate 大门　　ticket 门票　　lake 湖
tree 树木　　flower 花

> 你可以在公园里：

draw pictures 画画　　take photos 照相
fly kites 放风筝　　go boating 划船
go fishing 钓鱼　　go dancing 跳舞

8. My Hometown

May 5th   **Sunday**   **Sunshine**

I was born in Sydney. It is in the southeast of Australia. And it is a very big city.

The weather in Sydney is very good. In summer, it is much cooler than that in Shanghai. And it's warmer in winter. The best time for travel is in January. The most famous building is the Sydney Opera House.

I love my hometown.

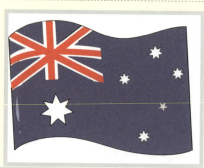

Places

UNIT 2

好词妙妙屋

southeast 东南方 weather 天气   Sydney 悉尼
summer 夏天   warm 温暖的   winter 冬天
travel 旅游   famous 著名的

be born in 出生在   the best time 最好的时间
Sydney Opera House 悉尼歌剧院

参考译文

5月5日　　　　　　星期日　　　　　　晴

　　我出生在悉尼，它位于澳大利亚的东南部。悉尼是一个非常大的城市。

　　悉尼的天气非常好。夏天，悉尼要比上海凉爽很多，冬天也更温暖。去悉尼旅游最好的时间是一月份。悉尼最著名的建筑是悉尼歌剧院。

　　我爱我的家乡。

语法小贴士

　　小朋友，我们已经学习了冠词 a 和 an 的用法，今天我们来认识一下冠词家族的另一位成员 the。请大家看看下面的例子，你们能发现什么规律吗？

the sun 太阳　　　the moon 月亮　　　the Great Wall 长城

A: Can you see a book? 你看见一本书了吗？
B: Is it the book on the desk? 是在桌子上的那本书吗？

冠词 the 可以表示世界上独一无二的物体，如：太阳、月亮、长城等；也可以用来特指上文提到的某一事物。

语法大擂台

读句子，选择合适的冠词。

a　　an　　the

1. I often eat _____ apple in the morning.
2. Do you know _____ Great Wall?
3. Every birthday, I receive _____ present from my parents.
4. Do you know _____ man with a hat?

Places

UNIT 2

日记导图秀

小朋友，你的家乡在哪里？你的家乡美吗？请你模仿上面的日记写一篇关于自己家乡的日记吧！

地点：Beijing, London

天气：warm, cold

My Hometown

...

名胜：the Forbidden City, Big Ben

_____ (DATE) _____ (DAY) _____ (WEATHER)

My Hometown

_____

_____

_____

_____

_____

参考范文

January 23rd   Friday   Windy

My Hometown

I was born in Harbin. It is in the northeast of China. And it is a very beautiful city.

The winter in Harbin is very cold. It always snows. In summer, it is very good, because it's not too hot. The most famous scenery in Harbin is its ice sculptures.

I love my hometown.

词汇加油站

▶ 描写天气：

warm 温暖的   cold 寒冷的
cool 凉爽的   hot 炎热的
humid 湿润的   dry 干旱的

▶ 描写城市：

modern 现代的   beautiful 美丽的
village 村庄   seaside 海滨

Places

9. A Trip in Hangzhou

| April 14th | Sunday | Sunny |

Yesterday I went to Hangzhou with my family. It was a terrible trip!

We got up very early in the morning, but our bus broke down. So we didn't catch the early train. When we arrived in Hangzhou, it was just raining. We didn't bring any umbrellas, so we all got wet.

What a bad trip!

好词妙妙屋

trip 旅行　　　　　　terrible 糟糕的　　　　　catch 赶上
train 火车　　　　　　arrive 到达　　　　　　bring 带来
umbrella 雨伞

get up 起床　　　　　　　　　　　　　break down 出故障了
get wet 湿透了

参考译文

4月14日　　　　　　星期日　　　　　　　　　晴

　　我们一家人昨天去杭州旅游了。这次旅游糟糕透了！

　　早上，我们很早就起床了，但是我们乘坐的公共汽车在路上坏了，所以我们没有赶上早班火车。当我们到达杭州的时候，杭州正在下雨。我们都没有带伞，因此我们都被淋湿了。

　　真是一次糟糕的旅行啊！

语法小贴士

　　小朋友们，我们前面已经学习了名词，我们知道，在一个名词前添加不同的修饰语，所得到的短语的意思也不同，我们把这些修饰名词的词叫作"形容词"。今天我们就来学习用形容词描述这个多彩的世界吧！

Places UNIT 2

描写心情

happy 开心的　　　　　angry 生气的
sad 伤心的　　　　　　excited 兴奋的
bored 无聊的　　　　　cheerful 高兴的
glad 高兴的　　　　　　disappointed 失望的
afraid 害怕的　　　　　worried 担心的

描写颜色

white 白色的　　　　　black 黑色的
green 绿色的　　　　　red 红色的
pink 粉色的　　　　　　blue 蓝色的
brown 棕色的　　　　　grey 灰色的
yellow 黄色的　　　　　purple 紫色的

描写天气

sunny 晴朗的　　　　　windy 多风的
rainy 下雨的　　　　　snowy 雪天的
cloudy 多云的　　　　　foggy 有雾的
hot 炎热的　　　　　　cold 寒冷的
humid 湿润的　　　　　dry 干旱的

　　形容词指表示名词的性质、颜色、大小和状态等的词语。形容词除了可以作定语修饰名词外，还可以作表语。

语法大擂台

读一读下面的单词，请把它们送回各自的家。

round	happy
tired	square
orange	sad
blue	thirsty
hungry	oval
green	excited

形状

颜色

感觉

心情

Places

UNIT 2

日记导图秀

小朋友，你去旅行过吗？都去过哪些城市？有什么经历呢？请你模仿上面的日记写一篇关于自己旅行的日记吧！

时间、地点：
...

交通：
crowded, traffic jam

A Trip in _____

特色：
beautiful sights, food

感受：
sad, happy

_____ (DATE)　_____ (DAY)　_____ (WEATHER)

A Trip in _____

_____
_____
_____
_____
_____

参考范文

July 25th   Friday   Sunny

A Trip in Sanya

  I went to Sanya with my family last summer. We had a happy holiday there!

  We went there by plane. When we arrived there, it was already noon. We had a good lunch. And then in the afternoon, we visited "Tianyahaijiao". It is very beautiful. Its name came from an ancient tale about a couple of lovers.

  What a pleasant trip!

词汇加油站

▶ 描写交通:

  take a bus / taxi 乘公共汽车 / 出租车
  crowded 拥挤的　　　　　traffic jam 交通堵塞
  red / green light 红 / 绿灯　narrow 窄的
  wide 宽的　　　　　　　bus stop 公交站

▶ 描写旅行:

  luggage 行李　　　　　　take photos 拍照
  go sightseeing 观光　　　 airport 机场
  passport 护照　　　　　　ticket 票
  travel / trip / journey 旅行

Places

UNIT 2

10. On My Way to School

October 15th   Tuesday   Cloudy

Today, I got up very early in the morning. After I finished the breakfast, I went to school.

On my way to school, I found an old man. He was lying on the road painfully. I called 120 at once, and helped the doctor send the old man to hospital. When I reached school, the class had begun. And I was late.

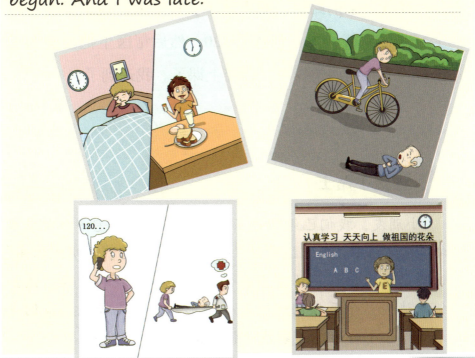

好词妙妙屋

finish 完成　　　breakfast 早餐　　　find 发现（过去式为 found）
lie 躺（现在分词为 lying）　　　painful 痛苦的
send 送　　　hospital 医院

on my way to school 上学路上　　　get up 起床
at once 立刻

参考译文

10月15日　　　　　星期二　　　　　多云

　　我今天早上起床很早。吃完早饭后，我就上学去了。
　　在我上学的路上，我发现了一位老人。他正躺在马路上，非常痛苦。我立刻打了120，然后帮医生把他送到了医院。当我到达学校时，已经上课了。我迟到了。

语法小贴士

　　小朋友，我们已经学习了如何用形容词描述一个人或事物。在汉语中，我们经常说"我比你跑得快""小明比你高"这样的话。但在英语中当我们想要表达比较的时候，该如何表达呢？今天我们就学习一下形容词的比较级。我们先来观察几个句子，大家找一找规律吧！

UNIT 2 Places

1. I am older than Amy. 我比艾米大。
2. My father is taller than my uncle. 我爸爸比叔叔高。
3. My shirt is cheaper than my shoes. 我的衬衫比鞋便宜。
4. This question is easier than that one. 这个问题比那个简单。
5. My mother is busier than my father on weekends.
   我妈妈在周末比爸爸忙。
6. My hat is more beautiful than his.
   我的帽子比他的帽子漂亮。
7. This movie is more interesting than that one.
   这部电影比那部电影有意思。

观察前三个例句，我们可以得到如下规律：
大多数形容词变成比较级的时候，通常在词尾加 -er。
观察第 4 个和第 5 个例句，我们可以得到如下规律：
一些以"辅音字母 +y"结尾的形容词变成比较级的时候，通常把 y 变成 i，再加 -er。
观察最后两个例句，我们可以得到如下规律：
一些音节比较多的形容词变成比较级的时候，通常在该形容词前加 more。

观察这几个例句，我们还发现，这几个例句都包含同一个单词"than"，在英语中表示比较通常都会用到这个词，意思为"比"。

这个单词在表达比较级时不可缺少哦！小朋友们，一定要记住哦！

语法大擂台

写出下列形容词的比较级。

1. wise 聪明的 _____
2. expensive 昂贵的 _____
3. tall 高的 _____
4. young 年轻的 _____
5. dirty 脏的 _____
6. delicious 美味的 _____

日记导图秀

小朋友，你在上学或放学回家的路上遇到过什么事情吗？请你模仿上面的日记写一篇关于自己上学或放学回家的路上所发生的事情的日记吧！

时间：morning, afternoon

如何做：call the policemen, send to hospital

On My Way (to) _____

看见的：a purse, a person

感受：happy

UNIT 2 Places

_____ (DATE) _____ (DAY) _____ (WEATHER)

On My Way (to)_____

_____
_____
_____
_____
_____

| June 5th | Wednesday | Sunny |

On My Way Home

After school, I went home on foot.

On the way, I found a purse. It was black with some money and several cards in it. I waited for the owner about half an hour, but he didn't appear. At last I gave it to a policeman. I got home late. My mother was very worried about me. After she heard the reason, she praised me.

I was very happy today, because I did a good thing.

词汇加油站

> 在路上还可能会发生：

  accident 事故　　　　traffic jam 堵车
  break down 出故障　　hurt 受伤
  wedding 结婚　　　　on fire 着火

> 在路上遇到突发事件还可以：

  call the ambulance / police / fireman
  叫救护车 / 警察 / 消防员

Unit 3

School Life

11. An Interesting English Class

April 23rd　　　　　Tuesday　　　　　Cloudy

　　Today, in the English class, our English teacher Miss Smith came into the classroom with a bag of fruits.

　　She asked us, "Can I help you?" No one answered her. After a while, I stood up and said, "I want some apples." Miss Smith praised me and gave me some apples.

　　I thought these apples were my awards. Do you think so?

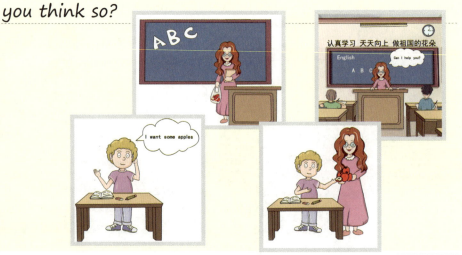

School Life

UNIT 3

好词妙妙屋

interesting 有趣的　　　fruit 水果　　　　answer 回答
want 想要　　　　　　　praise 表扬　　　award 奖品

a bag of 一袋　　　　　stood up 站起来

参考译文

4月23日　　　　　星期二　　　　　多云

　　今天英语课上，我们的英语老师史密斯女士带着一袋水果走进教室。

　　她问我们："我能帮你们吗？"没有人回答她。过了一会儿，我站了起来，说道："我想要一些苹果。"老师表扬了我，并给了我一些苹果。

　　我觉得这些苹果是我的奖品。你们也这样认为吗？

语法小贴士

　　多比来到中国学习了汉语之后发现，用汉语表达"最……"简直太简单了。他可以说"我最喜欢体育""莉莉最漂亮"等等。在英语中表示"最……"就比较复杂了。那么在英语中到底怎么表示"最……"的含义呢？我们来看一下以下几个例句。

1. Tony is the tallest boy in our class.
   托尼是我们班最高的男孩。

2. Russia is the largest country in the world.
   俄罗斯是世界上面积最大的国家。

3. This is my happiest day.
   这是我最高兴的一天。

4. Monday is the busiest day in a week.
   星期一是一周中最忙的一天。

5. My mother is the most beautiful woman in my mind.
   我妈妈在我心中是最漂亮的女士。

观察第 1 个和第 2 个例句，我们可以得到如下规律：

大多数形容词变成最高级的时候，通常在词尾加 -est；以不发音的字母 e 结尾的单词后加 -st。

观察第 3 个和第 4 个例句，我们可以得到如下规律：

一些以"辅音字母 +y"结尾的形容词变成最高级的时候，通常把 y 变成 i，再加 -est。

观察最后一个例句，我们可以得到如下规律：

一些多音节形容词变成最高级的时候，通常在该形容词前加 most。

观察这五个例句，我们还发现，有四个例句中的形容词的最高级前有定冠词 the；一个最高级前有形容词性物主代词。所以要记得哦！形容词最高级前要加定冠词 the 或形容词性物主代词哦！

UNIT 3

School Life

语法大擂台

根据图片提示，用所给单词的适当形式填空。

1. The red apple is _____ than the green one. (big)

2. The girl in red is _____ of the three girls. (beautiful)

3. The red rope is _____ than the blue one. (short)

4. The elephant is _____ than the monkey. (heavy)

日记导图秀

小朋友，你在学校里有喜欢的科目吗？请你模仿上面的日记写一篇关于一堂你喜欢的课的日记吧！

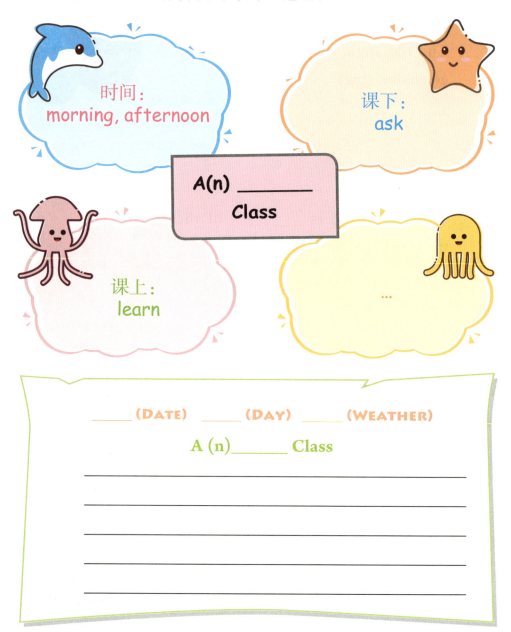

时间：morning, afternoon

课下：ask

A(n) _____ Class

课上：learn

...

_____ (DATE) _____ (DAY) _____ (WEATHER)

A (n) _____ Class

参考范文

May 5th   **Monday**   **Rainy**

A Special Science Class

This afternoon, we had a special science class. The teacher showed us many photos of animals. Some of the animals are in danger, such as pandas. And some died out, such as dinosaurs.

From the photos, we knew that we should stop killing animals and protect them.

词汇加油站

> 表示学校科目：

math 数学   Chinese 语文   history 历史
art 艺术   music 音乐   science 科学

> 描述科目内容：

meaningful 有意义的   important 重要的
boring 无聊的   funny 有趣的

12. Sports Meeting

April 29th   Monday   Sunny

Today, our school held a sports meeting. Many students took part in it.

Xiao Ming is good at running. He joined in the 100-meter race and won the first place. Fangfang likes swimming. She did very well in the swimming race.

I didn't join in any race, because I hurt my leg while playing football.

School Life

UNIT 3

好词妙妙屋

hold 举办（过去式为 held）　　race 比赛　　swim 游泳
hurt 受伤　　　　　　　　　　　leg 腿

sports meeting 运动会　　　　take part in 参加
be good at 擅长　　　　　　　join in 参加
do well in 在……做得好

参考译文

4月29日　　　　　　星期一　　　　　　晴

今天我们学校举办了运动会。很多学生都参加了。

肖明擅长跑步。他参加了100米赛跑，获得了第一名。

芳芳喜欢游泳。她在游泳比赛中取得了好成绩。

我什么比赛都没参加，因为我在踢足球时伤到了腿。

语法小贴士

小朋友，我们已经知道修饰名词要用形容词，那么修饰动词或形容词应该用什么呢？在汉语中，我们经常说"跑得快""跳得高""扔得远"，在英语中，也存在像"快""高""远"这样修饰动词的词，我们把它们叫作"副词"，副词可以用来修饰动词、形容词和副词本身。我们先看下面一组单词。

finally 最终　　carefully 小心地　　politely 有礼貌地
slowly 慢地　　badly 坏地　　happily 幸福地
easily 容易地　　usually 通常　　quickly 快速地

通过上面一组单词，我们发现

大多数副词都是以 -ly 结尾。

观察下面一组单词，看看有什么不同。

hard 努力地　　soon 不久　　ago 以前
downstairs 在楼下　　fast 快速地　　almost 几乎
just 只是　　then 之后　　already 已经

通过上面一组单词，我们发现

这些单词虽然不是以 -ly 结尾，但也是副词。这类副词主要有时间副词、地点副词和程度副词。

还有一些特别的单词也需要特殊记忆。

lovely 可爱的　　friendly 友好的　　likely 可能的

这些单词虽然以 -ly 结尾，却是形容词。

特别提示：我们在学习中经常用到的 so 和 very 也是副词哦！

语法大擂台

读一读下面的单词，请把它们送回各自的家。

friendly 友好的   lovely 可爱的

slowly 缓慢地   fast 快速地

happily 高兴地   likely 可能的

soon 不久   excited 兴奋的

weekly 每周的   easily 简单地

careful 小心的   heavily 重地

形容词

副词

日记导图秀

小朋友，你参加过学校组织的运动会吗？请你模仿上面的日记写一篇关于运动会的日记吧！

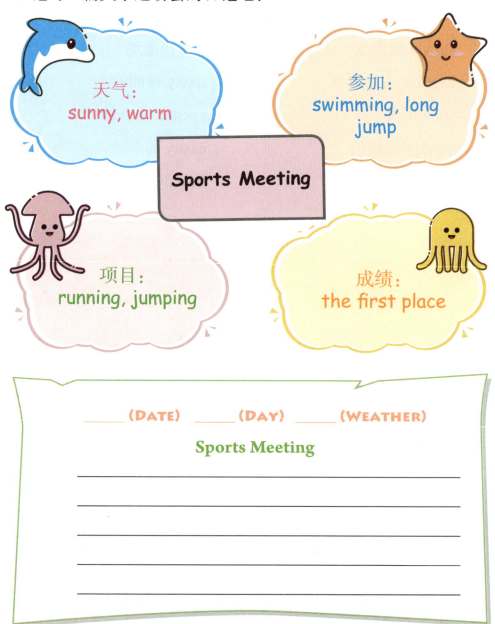

天气：sunny, warm

参加：swimming, long jump

Sports Meeting

项目：running, jumping

成绩：the first place

_____ (DATE) _____ (DAY) _____ (WEATHER)

Sports Meeting

_____
_____
_____
_____
_____

参考范文 12

May 15th   Friday   Sunny

Sports Meeting

In May, it's warm. Our school held a sports meeting.

There were many games, such as running, jumping, and ball games.

Half of my class joined in the meeting. Cindy often goes jogging in the morning, so she joined in the running. Tony joined in the high jump, and I joined in the swimming. All of us did very well.

Our class got the first place in the end. We were very happy.

词汇加油站

> 表示体育项目：

100-meter race 100 米赛跑   long jump 跳远
high jump 跳高   relay 接力

> 描写在运动会上的表现：

do very well 表现得非常好
make good results 取得好成绩
make a mistake 失误了
get the first / second place 获得第一 / 二名

13. The Tug of War

April 12th **Friday** **Sunny**

The school festival arrived. Our school held a tug of war this Friday!

There should be 10 boys and 10 girls in each team. We chose the strongest boys in our class to do it. When the competition began, we all tried our best to pull the rope. But unfortunately, we lost the game.

We were very disappointed.

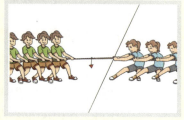

School Life
UNIT 3

好词妙妙屋

each 每个　　　　　strongest 最强壮的　　competition 比赛
pull 拉　　　　　　rope 绳子　　　　　　unfortunately 不幸地
lose 输掉（过去式为 lost）　　　　　　disappointed 失望的

tug of war 拔河比赛　　　　school festival 校园艺术节
try one's best 尽全力　　　　lose the game 比赛输了

参考译文

4月12日　　　　　星期五　　　　　　晴

校园艺术节到了。我们学校这周五举行了一场拔河比赛。

每个队伍都需要有10名男生和10名女生。我们选了班里最强壮的男生参加。比赛开始后，我们都尽全力拽绳子。不幸的是，我们输掉了比赛。

我们都很失望。

语法小贴士

小朋友，你知道英语里的 be 动词是什么吗？今天我们就来学习一下 be 动词的用法。be 动词意为"是"，有三种形式：am, are 和 is。下面我们就来看一下这三种形式的用法。

1. 当主语是第一人称单数，表示"我"时，be 动词要用 am。如：

   I am a student. 我是一名学生。

   I am 10 years old. 我 10 岁了。

2. 当主语是第二人称单数，表示"你"，或主语是复数时，be 动词要用 are。如：

   You are a teacher. 你是一名老师。

   We are good friends. 我们是好朋友。

   The students are playing football. 学生们正在踢足球。

3. 当主语是第三人称单数时，表示"他、她、它"时，be 动词要用 is。如：

   He is a driver. 他是一位司机。

   She is about 30 years old. 她 30 岁左右。

   It is a dog. 它是一条狗。

School Life

UNIT 3

语法大擂台

请找出小朋友的风筝。

 1.

 2.

 3.

A.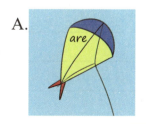

B.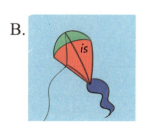

C.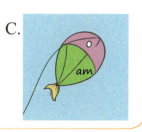

日记导图秀

小朋友，你参加过学校组织的各种比赛吗？请你模仿上面的日记写一篇关于比赛的日记吧！

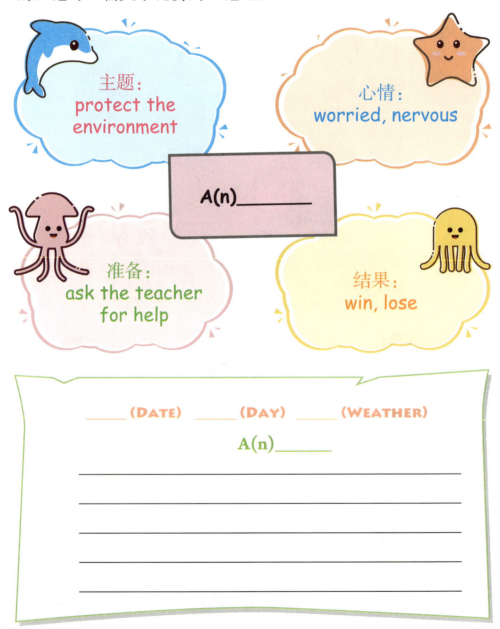

主题：protect the environment

心情：worried, nervous

A(n)_____

准备：ask the teacher for help

结果：win, lose

_____ (DATE) _____ (DAY) _____ (WEATHER)

A(n)_____

UNIT 3 School Life

| September 15th | Tuesday | Sunny |

An English Speech Contest

Today, I took part in an English speech contest.

Before the contest, I asked my English teacher to help choose the title. At last, we chose "How to protect the environment". When it was my turn, I was very nervous and worried. Unfortunately, I made some mistakes, and I didn't get into the final.

词汇加油站

> 描写比赛前的心情：

confident 自信的　　nervous 紧张的
afraid 害怕的　　　frightened 害怕的

> 描写准备比赛可以用：

practice speaking English 练习说英语
ask the teacher for help 寻求老师的帮助
choose the topic 挑选主题

14. A Painting Exhibition

May 22nd   **Wednesday**   **Cloudy**

Children's Day is coming. There will be a painting exhibition in our school.

We can bring our favorite painting. We can also draw our own paintings. My best friend Xiao Ming draws a tiger. It is very vivid. I can't draw very well, so I bring a painting of the West Lake. My father drew it.

We all like the paintings.

School Life

3 UNIT

好词妙妙屋

exhibition 展览　　　favorite 最喜欢的　　　draw 画画
tiger 老虎　　　　　vivid 生动的

Children's Day 儿童节　　　our own 我们自己的
the West Lake 西湖

参考译文

5月22日　　　　　星期三　　　　　多云

儿童节就要到了。我们学校将有一场绘画展。

我们可以带着我们最喜欢的画参加，也可以自己画画。我最好的朋友肖明画了一只老虎。画里的老虎栩栩如生。我不太会画画，所以带了一张西湖的图画，这张画是我爸爸画的。

我们都很喜欢这些图画。

语法小贴士

小朋友们，我们前面已经初步了解了 be 动词的用法，be 动词可以表示"是"或"有"。那么当我们想要说"不是"或"没有"时该如何表达呢？今天我们就来学习 be 动词的否定和疑问形式。

表达"否定"意义时，我们要借助 not，把 not 放在 be 动词后面。如：

I'm a student. 我是一名学生。

→ I'm not a student. 我不是一名学生。

There is a book on the desk. 桌子上有一本书。

→ There isn't a book on the desk. 桌子上没有书。

be 动词的疑问形式就是将 be 动词放在主语的前面，肯定回答用"Yes, 主语 + be 动词"，否定回答用"No, 主语 + be 动词 + not"。如：

Mary is a nurse. 玛丽是一名护士。

→ Is Mary a nurse? 玛丽是一名护士吗？

肯定回答：Yes, she is. 是的，她是。

否定回答：No, she isn't. 不，她不是。

特别提示：当句子中含有第一人称时，变疑问句时要将第一人称改为第二人称。

语法大擂台

按要求改写句子。

1. These dancers are from England.（改为否定句）

   These dancers are _____ from England.

2. My mother is going to have a meeting on Monday.（改为疑问句）

   _____ mother going to have a meeting on Monday?

   做肯定回答：_____, she _____.

   做否定回答：_____, she _____.

School Life

3 UNIT

日记导图秀

小朋友，你的学校或班级都举办过哪些活动？请你模仿上面的日记写一篇关于一次集体活动的日记吧！

参考范文

| October 21st | Wednesday | Sunny |

A Reading Party

Yesterday, our head teacher wanted to hold a reading party. She hoped we can learn more knowledge. She asked us to bring some books to school.

Today, all of us brought some books. There are story books, cartoon books, scientific books and so on. We shared with each other, and learned a lot.

We were very happy, and looked forward to the next activity.

词汇加油站

▶ 表示集体活动的单词或短语：

picnic 野餐　　　　　　climb the mountain 爬山
football / basketball match 足球 / 篮球比赛
Art Festival 艺术节

▶ 描写集体活动还可能用到：

take part in 参加　　　　join 加入
choose 选择　　　　　　all kinds of 各种各样的
visit museum / zoo 参观博物馆 / 动物园

School Life

UNIT 3

15. Spring Outing

| April 19th | Friday | Sunny |

  Today is very fine. Our class had a spring outing in the city park.

  We met together at the school gate at 7 am. When we arrived at the park, we took a photo together. In the park, we played games, flew kites, went fishing and so on. At noon, we had a picnic in the park. At about 3 pm, we went home.

  We had a very happy day!

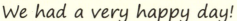

好词妙妙屋

meet 集合　　　　together 一起　　　　arrive 到达
noon 中午　　　　picnic 野餐

spring outing 春游　　　school gate 学校大门
take a photo 拍照　　　 fly kites 放风筝
go fishing 钓鱼

参考译文

> 4月19日　　　　星期五　　　　　　　晴
>
> 　　今天天气非常好。我们班去市公园春游了。
>
> 　　我们上午7点在学校大门集合。到了公园之后，我们拍了张合影。在公园里，我们做游戏、放风筝、钓鱼等。中午，我们在公园里野餐了。下午3点，我们回家了。
>
> 　　我们度过了非常愉快的一天！

语法小贴士

　　在汉语中，我们表达时间时，只要在时间的前面加上"在"就可以了，但是英语就没有这么简单了，不同的时间要用不同的介词，最常用的表示时间的介词有：in, on 和 at。今天我们主要介绍一下这三个介词的用法。

School Life

3 UNIT

1. I was born in March. 我在三月出生。
2. We often go skating in winter. 我们通常在冬天滑冰。
3. I do my homework in the evening. 我在晚上做作业。
4. Beijing Olympic Games were held in 2008.
   北京奥林匹克运动会在 2008 年举行。

观察以上四个例句，我们发现

介词 in 常用于表示年、季节、月及上午、下午、晚上的时间前。

5. We have a music class on Tuesday. 我们星期二有音乐课。
6. My father was born on December 3rd.
   我爸爸出生于 12 月 3 日。
7. I lost my purse on a cold morning.
   在一个寒冷的早上，我把钱包弄丢了。

观察以上三个例句，我们发现

介词 on 常用于表示星期、日期及具体哪一天的上午、下午、晚上的时间前。

8. I go to bed at 9 every evening. 我每天晚上都在 9 点睡觉。
9. At noon, we had a picnic in the park.
   中午，我们在公园里野餐了。

观察以上两个例句，我们发现

介词 at 常用于表示具体时刻的时间及 noon 和 night 前。

语法大擂台

为下列时间名词找到属于自己的家吧。

morning 上午　　　　　　　　night 晚上

Monday 星期一　　　　　　　October 十月

3:30　　　　　　　　　　　　spring 春天

a rainy afternoon 一个下雨的下午

in

on

at

UNIT 3 School Life

日记导图秀

小朋友，你参加过春游或秋游吗？请你模仿上面的日记写一篇关于春游或秋游的日记吧！

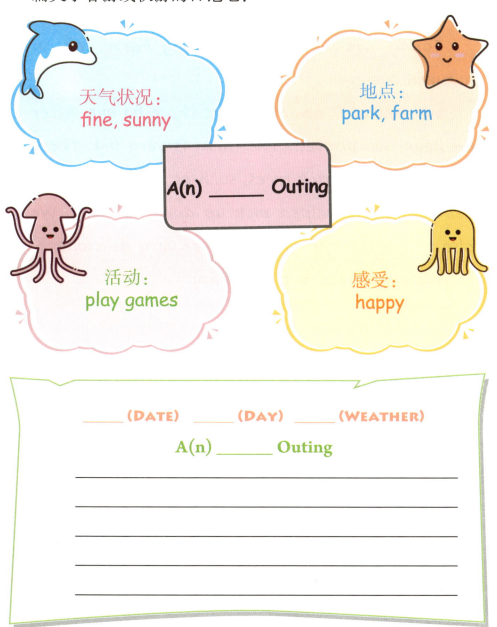

天气状况：fine, sunny

地点：park, farm

A(n) _____ Outing

活动：play games

感受：happy

_____ (DATE) _____ (DAY) _____ (WEATHER)

A(n) _____ Outing

参考范文 15

| October 12th | Saturday | Sunny |

An Autumn Outing

Today, we went to Hongxing Farm for an autumn outing.

We met at 7 am and went there by bus. After an hour, we arrived. The farm is very big. There are all kinds of fruit trees, such as apple trees and pear trees. We helped pick up apples all day. We also tasted the apples. They were very delicious.

We were tired but very happy.

词汇加油站

> 春游或秋游还可以去：

amusement park 游乐场　　zoo 动物园
botanical garden 植物园　　mountain 山
village 乡村　　　　　　　river bank 河边

Unit 4

Trips

16. I Went to Harbin

| August 11th | Tuesday | Snowy |

    This winter holiday I went to Harbin with my family.

    It was so cold there. People all wore thick coats, gloves and hats. There was snow everywhere. This was my first time to see the snow. I was very happy. My father helped me make a snowman. And I had a photo with it.

Trips

UNIT 4

好词妙妙屋

cold 寒冷的　　　　thick 厚的　　　　coat 外套
gloves 手套　　　　snowman 雪人

winter holiday 寒假　　　　　　make a snowman 堆雪人
This is my first time to do... 这是我第一次做……

参考译文

8月11日　　　　　星期二　　　　　　雪

今年寒假，我和家人一起去了哈尔滨。

哈尔滨非常冷。所有人都穿厚外套、戴手套和帽子。

街道上到处都是雪。这是我第一次看见雪。我非常开心。

我爸爸帮我堆了个雪人。我和雪人照了张相片。

语法小贴士

小朋友，我们已经知道在表示年、月、季节等的时间前用介词 in，在表示日期、星期等的时间前用介词 on，在表示具体时刻的时间前用介词 at。那么，你们知道如何表达具体的时刻吗？今天我们就来学习一下具体时刻的表达。

1. 表示整点，我们可以用 o'clock。如：

   8 o'clock 8 点　　　　　　　　12 o'clock 12 点

   其中，o'clock 可以省略。

   We have classes at 8. 我们在 8 点上课。

2. 表示几点过几分，用 past。如：

   five past three 3 点 5 分　　　　twenty past ten 10 点 20 分

   past 通常用于半点以前的时间。

   —What's the time? 几点了？

   —It's ten past nine. 9 点 10 分了。

3. 表示半点，可以用 half。如：

   half past seven 7 点半

   I go to bed at half past nine in the evening. 我晚上 9 点半睡觉。

4. 如果时间超过半点，用 to，to 前边的时间用 60 减去分钟的时间，to 后边的时间用时钟加 1，表示差几分到几点。如：

   ten to ten 9 点 50 分　　　　　five to six 5 点 55 分

   —What's the time? 几点了？

   —It's two to two. 1 点 58 分。

5. 表示一刻钟，可以用 quarter。如：

   a quarter past five 5 点 15 分　　a quarter to five 4 点 45 分

   I go home at a quarter to five every weekday.

   在上学日，我 4 点 45 分回家。

Trips

UNIT 4

语法大擂台

读一读下面的时间，找出与其相对应的钟表，并连线。

1. twenty past one   A.

2. half past nine   B.

3. a quarter past seven   C.

4. ten to nine   D.

5. three o'clock   E.

日记导图秀

小朋友,你在假期游览过哪些地方?给你印象深刻的是哪里?请你模仿上面的日记写一篇关于旅游的日记吧!

_____ (Date) _____ (Day) _____ (Weather)

I Went to _____

UNIT 4 Trips

参考范文

June 1st   Saturday   Sunny

I Went to the Zoo

Today is Children's Day. My parents took me to the zoo.

We went there by car. When we got to the zoo, there were many people. We first went to see the pandas. They were very cute. And then we saw monkeys, elephants, peacocks, lions and tigers. Monkeys were my favorite, because they were very clever.

We were very happy. I hope to come next year.

词汇加油站

> 动物园里的动物还有:

giraffe 长颈鹿   bear 熊
camel 骆驼   hippo 河马
dolphin 海豚   kangaroo 袋鼠

17. How to Travel

July 20th　　　　　**Saturday**　　　　　**Sunny**

　　Summer holiday arrived. I wanted to have a trip to Beijing. And I wanted to visit the Great Wall.

　　We didn't decide how to go there. My father wanted to take the plane, because it was fast. But my mother wanted to take the train. She thought the train was also very fast, and it was safe. I agreed with my mother, because I can walk on the train freely.

　　At last, we decided to take the train to Beijing.

UNIT 4 Trips

好词妙妙屋

arrive 到达　　　decide 决定　　　fast 快的
safe 安全的　　　walk 走路　　　　freely 自由地

how to travel 如何旅行　　　　have a trip 去旅行
the Great Wall 长城
take the plane / train 乘飞机 / 火车　　　agree with 同意

参考译文

7月20日　　　　星期六　　　　　　　晴

暑假到了。我想去北京旅游，我想去参观长城。

我们还没有决定如何去北京。爸爸想要乘飞机去，因为飞机很快。但是妈妈想要乘火车。她认为火车也很快，而且还安全。我同意妈妈的意见，因为我可以在火车上自由地行走。

最后我们决定乘火车去北京。

语法小贴士

小朋友，我们在前面学习了表示时间的介词，知道了如何表达时间。那么，你们知道如何表达地点吗？表示地点用哪些介词呢？我们常见的表示地点的介词有：in, on, under, behind。

in 表示"在……里"。如图：

My mother is cooking in the kitchen.
我妈妈在厨房做饭。
My pencil is in the pencil-box. 我的铅笔在铅笔盒里。
The cat is in the box. 小猫在纸盒里。

on 表示"在……上"。如图：

The boy is standing on the chair.
这个男孩正站在一把椅子上。
The book is on the desk. 书在桌子上。
There is a dog on the bed. 床上有一只小狗。

under 表示"在……下面"。如图：

There is a football under the bed.
床底下有一个足球。
My sister is sitting under a tree. 我姐姐正坐在树底下。
The cat is lying under the desk. 小猫正躺在书桌下。

behind 表示"在……后面"。如图：

My brother is hiding behind the door.
我弟弟藏在门后。
Linda stands behind me. 琳达站在我后面。
There is a boy behind the tree. 树后有一个男孩。

Unit 4 Trips

语法大擂台

根据图片，完成下列句子。

1. Look at the boy! He is playing _____ the tree.

2. The dog is _____ the bed. It is my pet.

3. This is my father. He is working _____ the study.

4. Look at the picture. There is a boy _____ the door.

日记导图秀

小朋友，你的假期有出游的计划吗？你打算去哪里游玩呢？请你以日记的形式描述一下吧！

时间：Spring Festival, summer vacation

建议：Hong Kong, Thailand...

Where to Travel

地点：didn't decide

最终决定

_____ (DATE) _____ (DAY) _____ (WEATHER)

Where to Travel

UNIT 4 Trips

参考范文 🎧 17

January 31st　　**Saturday**　　**Sunny**

Where to Travel

This Spring Festival, my family decided to have a trip. But we didn't decide where to go.

My father wanted to go to Harbin. He wanted to ski. My mother and I thought Harbin was too cold in winter, so we wanted to go to a warmer place. I wanted to go to Hainan and my mother wanted to go to Thailand.

At last we decided to go to Thailand, because my mother is the only lady in my family.

词汇加油站

> 描写旅游的好去处:

　　seaside 海边　　　beach 沙滩
　　mountain 山脉　　waterfall 瀑布

> 在旅游景点可以:

　　enjoy the sunshine and delicious food 享受阳光和美食
　　take photos 拍照
　　enjoy the beautiful scenery 欣赏美景
　　buy souvenirs 购买纪念品

18. The Forbidden City

July 25th   **Thursday**   **Cloudy**

    Today, my family visited the Forbidden City. It was very great.

    It is one of the most famous buildings in the world. And it was the palace of Ming and Qing dynasties. Now the Forbidden City is a museum. We saw many ancient treasures. Before we went back, I bought some gifts for my friends.

    Today we had a good time.

Trips

UNIT 4

好词妙妙屋

great 壮观的　　　famous 著名的　　　palace 宫殿
dynasty 朝代　　　museum 博物馆　　　ancient 古老的
treasure 宝藏

the Forbidden City 故宫　　　have a good time 玩得开心
It is one of the most... 它是最……之一。

参考译文

7月25日　　　　星期四　　　　多云

今天我们一家人游览了故宫。它非常壮观。

它是世界上最著名的建筑之一，曾经是明清两代的皇宫。现在，故宫是一座博物馆。我们看到了许多古老的宝物。离开前，我给我的好朋友买了一些礼物。

我们今天玩得很开心。

语法小贴士

小朋友，我们已经学习了名词、代词、形容词、副词、冠词和介词，今天我们来学习一下英语最重要的一个成员——动词。我们先看几个例句。

1. I write homework every day. 我每天都写作业。
2. My mother likes cooking. 我妈妈喜欢烹饪。
3. Mary runs fast. 玛丽跑得快。

从以上三个句子，我们可以看出：

write, like 和 run 都有具体的含义，这种有具体含义，能表达一般动作的动词，我们称为实义动词。这样的动词还有：jump, fly, think, eat, drink 等。

4. Do you like bananas? 你喜欢香蕉吗？
5. Tom did not go to school today. 汤姆今天没去上学。

从以上两个句子，我们可以看出：

do 在这两个句子中没有具体的含义，在例4中，do 和 like 构成了疑问句，在例5中，did 和 not 构成了否定句。像这种没有具体含义，不能在句中单独使用，必须与实义动词连用的动词，我们称为助动词。

6. I can speak English well. 我能说好英语。
7. She must finish the work before 3. 她三点之前必须完成工作。
8. It might rain. 天快要下雨了。

从以上三个句子，我们可以看出：

can, must 和 might 都有具体的含义，但不能单独使用，要与实义动词连用。这类动词我们称为情态动词。这样的动词还有：may, should, will, would 等。

Trips

UNIT 4

语法大擂台

根据图片，完成句子。

1. Tony _____ high.

2. Linda _____ like eating bananas.

3. Amy _____ draw.

4. The boy _____ swim very well.

5. Look! My mother _____ dinner in the kitchen.

我的英语日记书 入门篇

日记导图秀

小朋友，你暑假出去旅行了吗？都去了哪里，游览了哪些景点？请你模仿上面的日记写一篇关于某个景点的日记吧！

位置：
London, Beijing

建成时间：
in...

外形：
tall

...

_____(DATE) _____(DAY) _____(WEATHER)

Unit 4 Trips

参考范文

August 21st   Saturday   Sunny

Big Ben

Last summer vacation, I went to London with my parents. We visited the Big Ben.

Big Ben is one of the landmarks of London. It was built in 1858. It was very tall and big. It was like a tower from far away. The Big Ben rang every an hour. Its name was changed to Elizabeth Tower in June in 2012.

词汇加油站

> 世界著名的建筑还有：

the Summer Palace 颐和园

the Great Wall 长城

White House 白宫

the Eiffel Tower 埃菲尔铁塔

the Pyramid 金字塔

19. I Got Lost!

August 2nd   **Friday**   **Sunny**

I had a very frightening day today. I got lost with my parents.

Today I went to the aquarium with my parents. After an hour's walk, I felt very thirsty. My father went to buy some drinks. My mother and I were sitting by the road. Several minutes later, I couldn't find my mother anywhere. I was very scared and I cried. Thanks to a policeman, he helped me find my parents.

Trips

UNIT 4

好词妙妙屋

frightening 害怕的   aquarium 海洋馆   thirsty 口渴的
several 几个   scared 害怕的

get lost 迷路了   by the road 在路边
thanks to 多亏   help sb. do sth. 帮助某人做某事

参考译文

8月2日　　　　　　星期五　　　　　　　晴

我度过了非常害怕的一天。我和爸爸妈妈走散了。

今天我和爸爸妈妈去了海洋馆。走了一个小时后，我感觉渴了。我爸爸去买饮料。我和妈妈坐在路边。几分钟以后，我找不到妈妈了。我害怕得哭了。多亏了一位警察，他帮助我找到了爸爸妈妈。

语法小贴士

小朋友，你们发现了吗？英语中有个特别任性的动词，它一会是实义动词，一会是助动词，一会是这个意思，一会是那个意思，没有特定的含义。这个动词就是 do。今天我们就来学习一下动词 do 的用法。

1. I will do my homework on Saturday. 我周六要做家庭作业。
2. I can do the job myself. 我自己可以做这项工作。

从以上两个句子，我们可以看出：
do 在这两个句子中是实义动词，表示一般动作，意为"做，干"。

3. I do not want to have lunch. 我不想吃午饭。

4. I do not know where to go. 我不知道去哪里。

从以上两个句子，我们可以看出：
do 在这两个句子中是助动词，用来构成否定句。

5. Do you know the boy with a hat? 你知道戴帽子的男孩是谁吗？

6. Do you want to join us? 你想加入我们吗？

从以上两个句子，我们可以看出：
do 在这两个句子中是助动词，用来构成疑问句。

此外，do 常和一些介词或名词搭配，构成短语。如：

do with 处理　　　　　　do harm to 对……有害
do one's best 尽力　　　　do one's duty 尽职责
have nothing to do with 与……无关

语法大擂台

读一读下面的句子，将动词 do 的用法进行分类。

A. Alice, do you have any stamps?

B. I didn't have breakfast this morning.

C. Did you enjoy yourself in London?

D. I did some housework on Sunday.

E. She doesn't listen to the teacher.

F. My mother always does housework on weekends.

实义动词	构成否定句	构成疑问句

Trips

日记导图秀

小朋友，你在旅行中有没有遇到过一些令你难忘的事情？请你模仿上面的日记描写一下吧！

_____ (Date)　_____ (Day)　_____ (Weather)

参考范文 19

| August 26th | Thursday | Sunny |

I Want to Be a Doctor

On the plane, an old man suddenly fell down. Luckily, there was a doctor. She looked over the old man carefully. About half an hour later, the old man woke. He thanked the doctor for saving his life.

I was moved very much. And I decided to be a doctor in the future.

词汇加油站

▶ 旅行中还有可能发生：

There was an accident on the road.
路上发生了交通事故。
I lost my bag / purse. 我弄丢了包 / 钱包。
I was trapped in traffic jam. 我遇上堵车了。
Our flight was put off. 我们的航班延误了。
On the plane, I met a famous star.
在飞机上，我遇见了一位明星。

20. Preparing for a Trip

| July 22nd | Monday | Rainy |

  This summer vacation, I will go to Beijing with my family.

  I made a plan. We will go to visit the Great Wall, the Summer Palace, the Palace Museum, the Bird Nest and the Water Cube. We will also prepare some clothes to protect our skin from sunburn.

  I hope we have a good time there.

好词妙妙屋

prepare 准备　　　　plan 计划　　　　skin 皮肤
sunburn 晒伤

summer vacation 暑假　　　　protect... from 保护……免受
have a good time 玩得开心

参考译文

7月22日　　　　星期一　　　　雨

　　今年暑假，我们一家人准备去北京。

　　我做了一个计划。我们要去参观长城、颐和园、故宫、鸟巢和水立方。我们还要准备一些衣服以免被晒伤。

　　我希望我们能玩得开心。

语法小贴士

　　小朋友，你知道如何用英语表达"我会游泳""我能弹钢琴"这些句子吗？其中的"会、能"该如何表达呢？这时候就需要情态动词can的帮忙了。今天我们就来学习一下情态动词can的用法。

Trips

UNIT 4

1. I can ride a bike. 我会骑自行车。

2. I can do the job by myself. 我自己可以做这项工作。

can 在这两个句子中表示能力，意为"能、会"。

3. I can't fly. 我不会飞。

4. I can't finish the homework on time. 我不能按时完成作业。

表示"不能、不会"的意思时，我们只需要在 can 的后边加上 not 就可以了，缩写为 can't。要注意一点：cannot 不可以分开哦！

5. Can I help you? 我能帮助你吗？

6. You can use my pencil. 你可以使用我的铅笔。

can 在这两个句子中表示请求或许可。Can I...? 用来征求对方是否允许自己做某事；Can you...? 表示说话人的请求。

7. Can the news be true? 这个消息会是真的吗？

8. The light is on. Tom can't sleep now.
   灯还亮着。汤姆不可能在睡觉。

can 在这两个句子中表示推测，意为"可能"，常与否定句和疑问句连用。

语法大擂台

根据图片，完成句子。

1. He _____ skate.

2. Tom _____ play the piano very well.

3. Nancy _____ sing well.

4. The boy _____ swim.

Unit 4 Trips

日记导图秀

小朋友，你做过旅行计划吗？请你模仿上面的日记写一下你的旅行计划吧！

_____ (DATE) _____ (DAY) _____ (WEATHER)

Preparing for a Trip

参考范文

December 23rd   Thursday   Sunny

Preparing for a Trip

This Christmas Day, I will visit London with my parents.

I will go to see the Big Ben, the London Eye and the Tower Bridge. I also want to have a ride on River Thames.

I hope to have a happy holiday.

词汇加油站

▶ 旅行前的准备工作：

book the tickets / hotel 预订车票 / 旅店

plan the routine 规划路线

what to bring / take 准备带的东西

where to have meal 就餐地点

Unit 5

Activities

21. My Day

April 12th **Friday** **Rainy**

I am usually busy every day.

I get up at half past six. I do some exercises before breakfast. I go to school at half past seven. I have three classes in the morning and two lessons in the afternoon. I go home at five. I do my homework after dinner. I often go to bed at half past nine.

Activities UNIT 5

好词妙妙屋

usually 通常　　busy 忙碌的　　before 在……之前
breakfast 早饭　　often 经常

get up 起床　　　　do exercises 锻炼
go to school 上学　go home 回家
go to bed 上床睡觉

参考译文

4月12日　　　　星期五　　　　雨

我通常每天都很忙。

我早上六点半起床，吃早饭前锻炼。我七点半去上学。我上午有三节课，下午有两节课。我下午五点回家，晚饭后做作业。我经常九点半上床睡觉。

语法小贴士

小朋友，我们经常在公共场所看到下面几个标识，你知道如何用英语表达吗？这就需要用到情态动词 must 了。今天我们就来学习一下 must 的用法。

1. I **must** finish my homework first. 我必须先完成家庭作业。
2. You **must** come home before nine. 你九点前必须回家。

must 在这两个句子中表示命令，意为"必须"，不可违抗。

3. The light is on. She **must** be at home. 灯还亮着，她一定在家。
4. You look tired. You **must** sleep late yesterday.
   你看起来很累，昨天你一定睡得很晚。

must 在这两个句子中表示推测，意为"一定"。

5. Look at this mark. You **mustn't** smoke here.
   看这个标识。这里禁止吸烟。
6. You **mustn't** take photos here. 这里禁止拍照。

mustn't 在这两个句子中表示禁止。

特别注意：回答 must 引起的一般疑问句，如果作否定回答，一般用 needn't，不能用 mustn't。如：

—Must I finish the homework today? 我必须今天完成作业吗？
—Yes, you must. 是的，你必须今天完成。（肯定）
　No, you needn't. 不，你不必今天完成。（否定）

Activities

UNIT 5

语法大擂台

读句子，将句子与其对应的标识连线。

1. You mustn't stop your car here.　　A.

2. You mustn't smoke on the bus.　　B.

3. You mustn't use your phone.　　C.

4. You mustn't turn left here.　　D.

5. You mustn't throw rubbish.　　E.

日记导图秀

小朋友，你一天的生活是什么样的？每天都会做什么？请你模仿上面的日记描写一下自己一天的生活吧！

总体状况：busy, easy

在校：have classes

My Day

在家：get up, have dinner

...

_____(DATE) _____(DAY) _____(WEATHER)

My Day

Unit 5 Activities

参考范文

September 23rd   Sunday   Sunny

My Day

Usually, I am a little busy. But today I was easy.

I didn't need to go to school, because today was Sunday. I got up at 8. In the morning, I did my homework. In the afternoon, I played football with my friends. In the evening, I watched TV for half an hour. I went to bed at 9.

词汇加油站

> 描写一天的活动还有：

play basketball / the piano / the guitar
打篮球 / 弹钢琴 / 弹吉他
I study English / Chinese / math.
我学习英语 / 语文 / 数学。
I go shopping / fishing. 我去购物 / 钓鱼。
After breakfast, I go to school. 早饭后我去上学。
I have six classes at school. 我今天有六节课。

22. A Football Match

May 18th   Saturday   Cloudy

Today, our school team had a football match with No. 5 Primary School.

At 3 o'clock, the game began. After half time, neither of us kicked a goal. In the other half, Xiao Ming helped our team kick a goal. In the end, we won the match.

We were very happy.

UNIT 5 Activities

好词妙妙屋

match 比赛　　　　neither 两者都不　　win 获胜

school team 校队　　half time 半场　　kick a goal 进球
in the end 最后

参考译文

5月18日　　　　　　星期六　　　　　　多云

今天我们校队和第五小学踢了一场足球比赛。

下午三点，比赛开始了。半场过后，两支球队都没有进球。在下半场，肖明帮助我们队踢进了一球。最后我们赢得了比赛。

我们非常高兴。

语法小贴士

我们在学习动词时，发现动词中有一个淘气的 do，而情态动词也有一个非常调皮的成员——will，它可以表达可能性，如：It will rain. 可能要下雨了。也可以表示将来要做的事，如：I will go to climb the hill next Sunday. 我下周日将要去爬山。今天我们就来学习一下 will 的用法。

will 表示可能性。

That animal will be an insect. 那只动物可能是一只昆虫。

This will be your book. 这个可能是你的书。

will 表示意愿。

No one will do that job. 没有人愿意做那份工作。

I will never go to that restaurant. 我再也不会去那家餐厅了。

will 表示将来要做的事。

I will have an English test tomorrow. 我明天有一个英语测试。

Will you be free this Sunday? 你这周日有时间吗?

特别注意：will 的过去式为 would，两者表达意思几乎相同，但是在表示"请求"时，would 更委婉客气。如：

Would you pass me the book? 您能把那本书递给我吗?

语法大擂台

读一读下面的句子，将情态动词 will 的用法进行分类。

A. Someone is at the door. It will be Jack.

B. Bob will leave school next month.

C. Will you accept the check?

D. I will take part in the sports meeting.

E. The car will hold six people.

F. Come whenever you will.

表示意愿	表示可能性	表示将来

Activities

UNIT 5

日记导图秀

小朋友,你参加或观看过篮球比赛吗?请你模仿上面的日记描写一场篮球比赛吧!

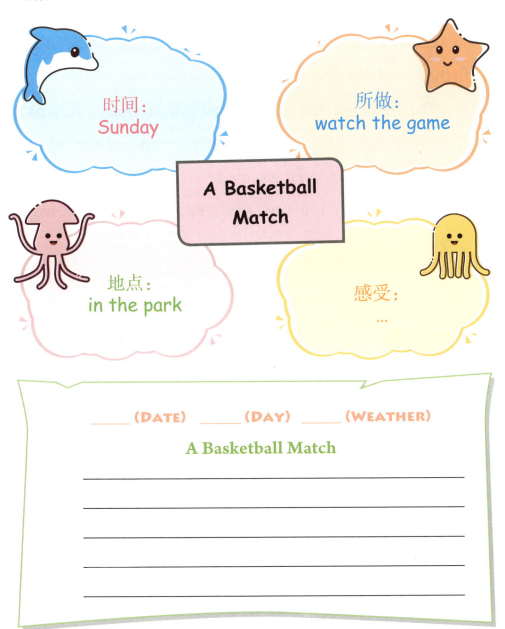

时间:Sunday

所做:watch the game

A Basketball Match

地点:in the park

感受:...

_____ (DATE) _____ (DAY) _____ (WEATHER)

A Basketball Match

_____
_____
_____
_____
_____

参考范文 22

October 24th　　　　Sunday　　　　Sunny

A Basketball Match

Last Sunday, I went to the park with my father and his friends.

They played the basketball game there. It was the first time for me to watch my father play basketball. I was very excited.

Since then, I often play basketball with my father.

词汇加油站

▶ 描写一次比赛可能会用到：

competition rules 比赛规则

score 比分

coach 教练

pass the ball 传球

Time's up. The game is over. 时间到，比赛结束。

23. Planting Trees

| March 12th | Tuesday | Sunny |

Today is Tree Planting Day. We went to the West Hill to plant trees.

Some students dug holes. Some put the trees into the holes. Some put the soil back to the holes. At last we watered the trees.

We hoped the trees would grow well.

好词妙妙屋

plant 种植　　　　dig 挖　　　　　　hole 坑
soil 土壤

plant trees 植树　　water the trees 给树浇水

参考译文

> 3月12日　　　　　星期二　　　　　　　晴
>
> 　　今天是植树节。我们去西山植树了。
>
> 　　有的同学挖坑，有的同学把小树放进坑里，还有的同学把土埋回坑里。我们最后给树苗浇水了。
>
> 　　我们希望这些树苗能茁壮成长。

语法小贴士

　　小朋友们，你们知道如何表达不确定的事物吗？当你对一件事不是特别肯定的时候，你知道该用哪些表达方式吗？今天我们就来学习一下 may 的用法。

UNIT 5 Activities

may 表示可能性，意为"也许，可能"。当你对某件事情不是特别肯定的时候，你就可以用 may。

Jack didn't come to school today. He may be ill.
杰克今天没来上学，他可能生病了。

Tom didn't answer my call. He may be busy.
汤姆没有接我的电话，他可能在忙。

may 表示许可。

You may use my car. 你可以开我的车。

You may go now. 你现在可以走了。

May 放在句首，构成疑问句时，表示委婉请求。

May I come in? 我可以进来吗？

May I use your computer? 我可以用一下你的电脑吗？

语法大擂台

读一读下面的句子，根据图片补全句子。

1. You look tired. You may _____.

2. May I use your _____? Mine is broken.

3. I may take you to the _____.

日记导图秀

小朋友，你参加过保护环境的活动吗？请你模仿上面的日记描述一下吧！

_____(DATE) _____(DAY) _____(WEATHER)

Living a Low-carbon Life

UNIT 5 Activities

| April 26th | Friday | Sunny |

Living a Low-carbon Life

Today we had a lesson about protecting the environment.

Now, the air pollution is very serious. The teacher asked us to do something. I won't ask my father to take me to school. I will take the bus.

I hope everyone will take actions to protect our earth.

> 描写环境保护的措施还有：

save water 节约用水

Don't use plastic bags. 不要使用塑料袋。

Don't throw rubbish everywhere. 不要到处扔垃圾。

24. Preparing for Christmas

| December 22nd | Sunday | Snowy |

Christmas Day is coming. My family decided to invite some friends.

This morning we cleaned the house. Mother swept the floor. Father cleaned the window. I helped make the invitation cards.

This afternoon, we went to the supermarket. We bought some lights, gifts and a turkey.

Unit 5 Activities

好词妙妙屋

invite 邀请
supermarket 超市

sweep 扫地
turkey 火鸡

Christmas Day 圣诞节
invitation card 邀请函

clean the house 打扫房间

参考译文

12月22日　　　　星期日　　　　　　　　雪

圣诞节就要到了。我们决定邀请一些朋友。

今天上午，我们打扫了房间。妈妈扫地，爸爸擦玻璃，我帮着制作邀请函。

今天下午，我们去了超市。我们买了一些彩灯、礼品和一只火鸡。

语法小贴士

小朋友们，我们在生活中经常听到"你应该多吃蔬菜""你应该多锻炼""我应该早点睡觉"这样的话，但你知道用英语如何表达吗？今天我们就来学习一下情态动词的另一个成员——should。

should 表示意愿，常与第一人称连用，意为"应该"。

I should do my homework first. 我应该先做作业。

We should give our seats to the old on the bus.
在公交车上我们应该给老人让座。

should 可以表示给别人提建议。

You should take more exercises. 你应该多运动。

You should get up earlier next morning.
你明天早上应该早点起床。

should not 或 shouldn't 是 should 的否定形式，表示"不应该"。

You shouldn't sleep so late. 你不应该那么晚睡觉。

You shouldn't take my book without my permission.
没有我的许可，你不应该拿我的书。

语法大擂台

读一读下面的句子，根据图片补全句子。

1. I should buy some _____ on Mother's Day.

2. You shouldn't play _____ on the street.

3. You cough so seriously. You should _____.

Activities

UNIT 5

日记导图秀

小朋友，你在春节前都会准备些什么？请你模仿上面的日记描写一下吧！

介绍：
Spring Festival comes...

春节：
have a big meal

Preparing for Spring Festival

春节前：
clean house, shopping

...

_____(Date) _____(Day) _____(Weather)

Preparing for Spring Festival

_____
_____
_____
_____
_____

参考范文

| February 4th | Friday | Sunny |

Preparing for Spring Festival

Spring Festival is coming. It usually comes in January or February.

Before Spring Festival, we will clean our house and go shopping. On the day, we will set off fireworks and have a big meal. Children will also get lucky money from the old.

词汇加油站

▶ 表示中外的节日还有：

Mid-Autumn Festival 中秋节
Dragon Boat Festival 端午节
Thanksgiving Day 感恩节
Halloween 万圣节前夕

▶ 庆祝节日还可能准备：

delicious food 美食
couplets 春联
greeting card 贺卡
visit relatives and friends 拜访亲戚和朋友

25. I Can Shop

July 20th   Saturday   Sunny

This noon, my mother was cooking lunch. She found the soy run out. She asked me to buy a bottle. I have never bought anything on my own. I was a little nervous. There were many kinds of soy in the shop. At last I chose one.

It was my first time to shop on my own. I was very happy.

好词妙妙屋

cook 做饭
never 从不

soy 酱油
nervous 紧张的

run out 用光了
a little 有点
It is my first time to do... 这是我第一次……

on one's own 独自

参考译文

7月20日　　　　　星期六　　　　　晴

　　今天中午我妈妈正在做午饭。她发现酱油用完了。她让我去超市买一瓶。我从来没有独自买过东西，我有点紧张。超市里有很多种酱油。最后我选了一种。

　　这是我第一次独自买东西。我非常高兴。

语法小贴士

　　前面我们学习了情态动词 should 的用法，掌握了 should 意为 "应该" 时的用法。我们在阅读时也经常遇到 "I have to do my homework." 这样的句子，这里的 have to 也是情态动词的一种。今天我们就来学习一下 have to 的用法。

Activities

UNIT 5

have to 表示客观上必须,意为"不得不"。当你不情愿做某事,却又不得不做时,你就可以用 have to。

I have to prepare for the English test. I can't go with you.
我得准备英语考试。我不能和你去。

I have to finish my homework before 5 pm.
我得在下午 5 点前做完作业。

have to 有人称和数的变化,当主语是第三人称单数时,用 has to。

My mother's car broke down. She has to go to work by bus.
我妈妈的汽车坏了。她只好乘公交车去上班。

语法大擂台

读一读下面的句子,根据图片补全句子。

1. It is _____. I _____ stay at home.

2. I can't go to the party. I _____ do my homework.

3. My father got up late. He _____ take the taxi to work.

我的英语日记书 入门篇

日记导图秀

小朋友，你还记得你第一次独立完成一件事情（如游泳）的经过吗？请你模仿上面的日记描写一下吧！

_____ (DATE) _____ (DAY) _____ (WEATHER)

I Can Swim

_____
_____
_____
_____
_____

参考范文 25

| June 24th | Saturday | Sunny |

I Can Swim

My father will take me to the seaside. I want to swim in the sea. But I can't swim.

I took part in a lesson to learn to swim. A week later, I tried to swim. I was afraid at first. After several tries, I can swim. I was very happy.

词汇加油站

> 描写"我会……"还有:

ride a bike 骑自行车

play football / basketball / tennis
踢足球 / 打篮球 / 打网球

play the piano / guitar / violin
弹钢琴 / 弹吉他 / 拉小提琴

参考答案

Unit 1　My Family and Friends

1 This Is Me!
语法大擂台

可数名词：bag, book, cake, pencil, cap, cat

不可数名词：rain, snow, water, tea, money, ice

2 My Family
语法大擂台

bananas　cars　pens　erasers　eyes　shoes　doors　oranges　books　pictures　computers　heads

3 My Grandpa's Birthday
语法大擂台

加 -s：monkey, friend, cake, sport, holiday

变 y 为 i，再加 -es：lady, cherry

加 -es：bus, match, dress, toothbrush

变 f 或 fe 为 v，再加 -es：wife, shelf, thief, life

4 My Best Friend—Xiao Ming
语法大擂台

1—C　2—A　3—E　4—D　5—B

5 Teachers' Day
语法大擂台

1. She　2. They　3. He　4. I　5. we　6. It

Unit 2 Places

6 My Room

语法大擂台

1. This 2. Those 3. That 4. These

7 On the Farm

语法大擂台

a: grape   corn   map   tomato   lion   tree

an: orange   airplane   ear   elephant   actor   ant

8 My Hometown

语法大擂台

1. an 2. the 3. a 4. the

9 A Trip in Hangzhou

语法大擂台

形状：round   square   oval

颜色：orange   blue   green

感觉：tired   thirsty   hungry

心情：happy   sad   excited

10 On My Way to School

语法大擂台

1. wiser 2. more expensive 3. taller 4. younger

5. dirtier 6. more delicious

Unit 3　School Life

⑪ An Interesting English Class

语法大擂台

1. bigger　2. the most beautiful　3. shorter　4. heavier

⑫ Sports Meeting

语法大擂台

形容词：friendly　lovely　likely　excited　weekly　careful

副词：slowly　fast　happily　soon　easily　heavily

⑬ The Tug of War

语法大擂台

1. C　2. A　3. B

⑭ A Painting Exhibition

语法大擂台

1. not　2. Is your; Yes; is; No; isn't

⑮ Spring Outing

语法大擂台

in：morning　October　spring

on：Monday　a rainy afternoon

at：night　3:30

Unit 4　Trips

16 I Went to Harbin
语法大擂台
1. C　2. D　3. A　4. E　5. B

17 How to Travel
语法大擂台
1. under　2. on　3. in　4. behind

18 The Forbidden City
语法大擂台
1. jumps　2. doesn't　3. can　4. can　5. is cooking

19 I Got Lost!
语法大擂台
实意动词：D　F
构成否定句：B　E
构成疑问句：A　C

20 Preparing for a Trip
语法大擂台
1. can　2. can　3. can't　4. can't

Unit 5　Activities

21 My Day
语法大擂台
1—C　2—D　3—E　4—A　5—B

22 A Football Match
语法大擂台

表示意愿：C　F

表示可能性：A　E

表示将来：B　D

23 Planting Trees
语法大擂台

1. sleep late　2. bike　3. supermarket

24 Preparing for Christmas
语法大擂台

1. flowers　2. football　3. go to see the doctor

25 I Can Shop
语法大擂台

1. raining; have to　2. have to　3. has to